I'm Just Like You

By: Semaj Lopez

Copyright © 2022 Maria Lopez

All rights reserved.

ISBN: 979-8-218-05046-7

This book is dedicated to anyone who ever felt different. Everyone is born unique and comes from different walks of life; it is okay to ask for help.

My name is Semaj Lopez. I was born with hearing loss, and for as long as I can remember I wore hearing aids. I never really understood the purpose of wearing hearing aids, but as I got older I realized they were needed to help me communicate, hear, and grow.

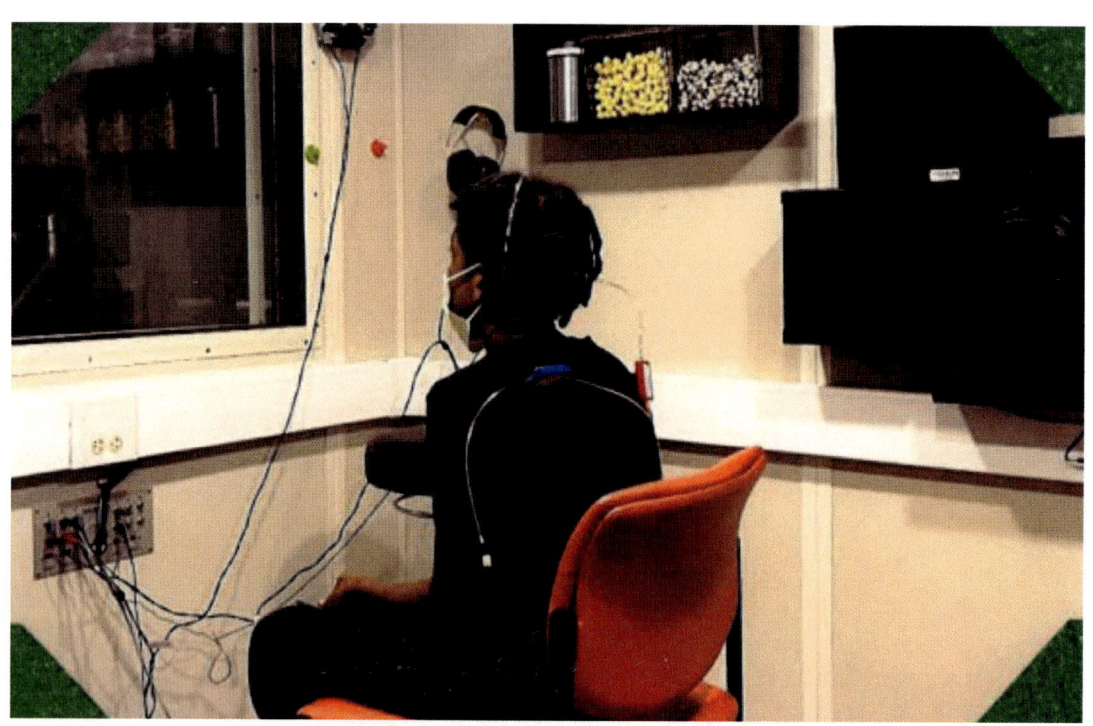

When I was four years old my audiologist ran me through a couple of hearing tests to learn the extent of my hearing loss. I was taken into a soundproof room and was presented with speech and word recognition tests. It showed how well I could hear spoken language.

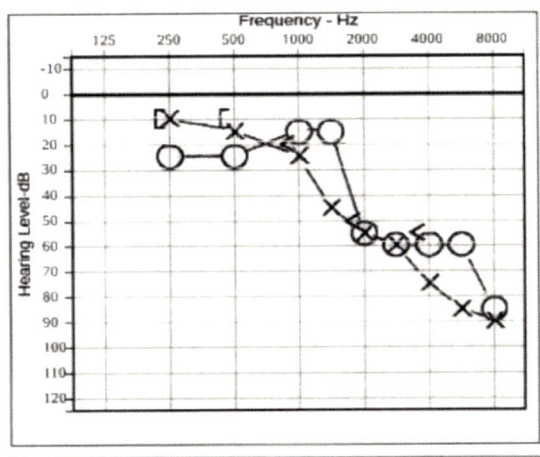

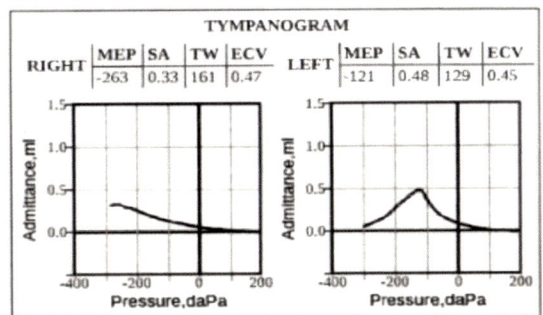

MIDDLE EAR TEST

I was also given a middle-ear test to check my eardrum movement. After the tests were completed, I was diagnosed with moderate hearing loss and speech impairment. I could not hear certain sounds, such as tones that were too high or too low.

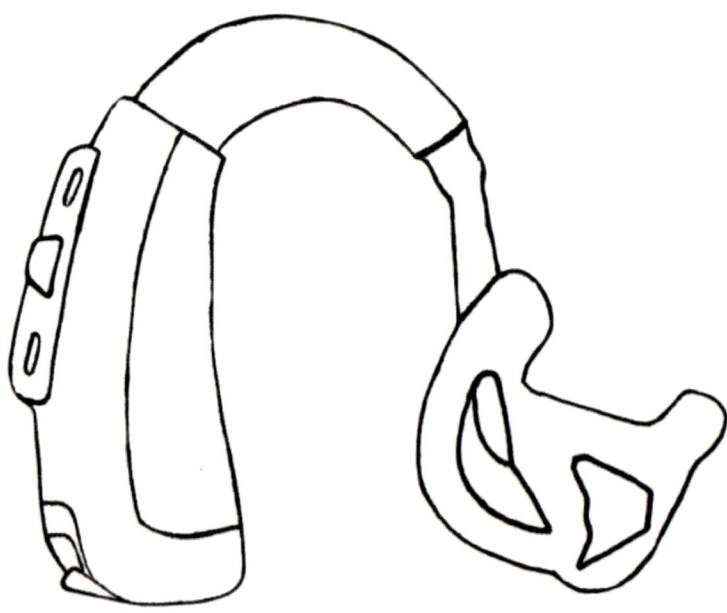

HEARING AID

To better assist me, the audiologists requested to my mother that I wear hearing aids on both ears. A hearing aid is a device that is worn either behind or inside the ear. The hearing aid amplifies (makes louder) sound. A hearing aid has three basic parts: a microphone, the amplifier, and a speaker.

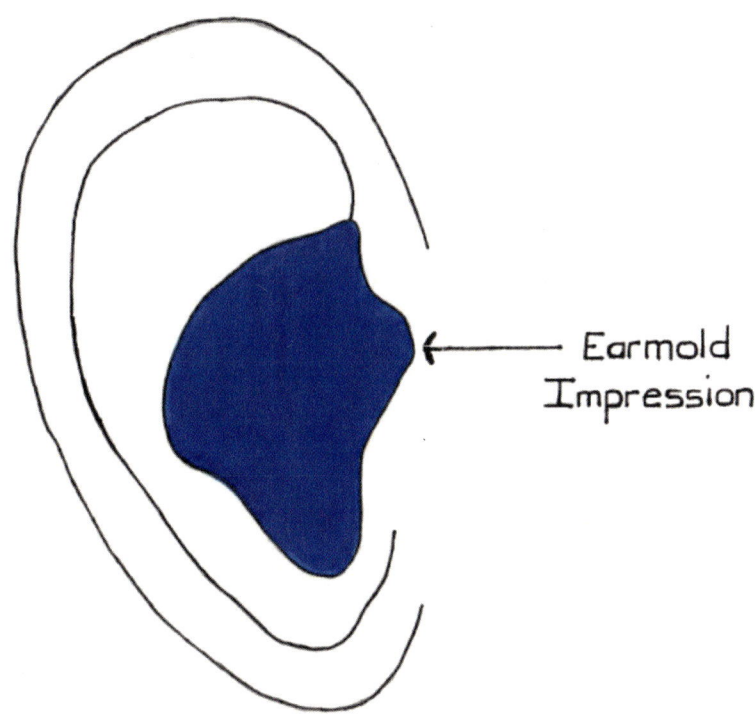

The making of the hearing aids took a couple of weeks. First, I got ear molds made for both my ears. My ear canal was filled with a kind of wax for a couple of minutes to get an impression of my ears. Then, I was given the chance to pick out colors for my devices. Finally, I had to wait a couple of weeks to receive my new hearing aids.

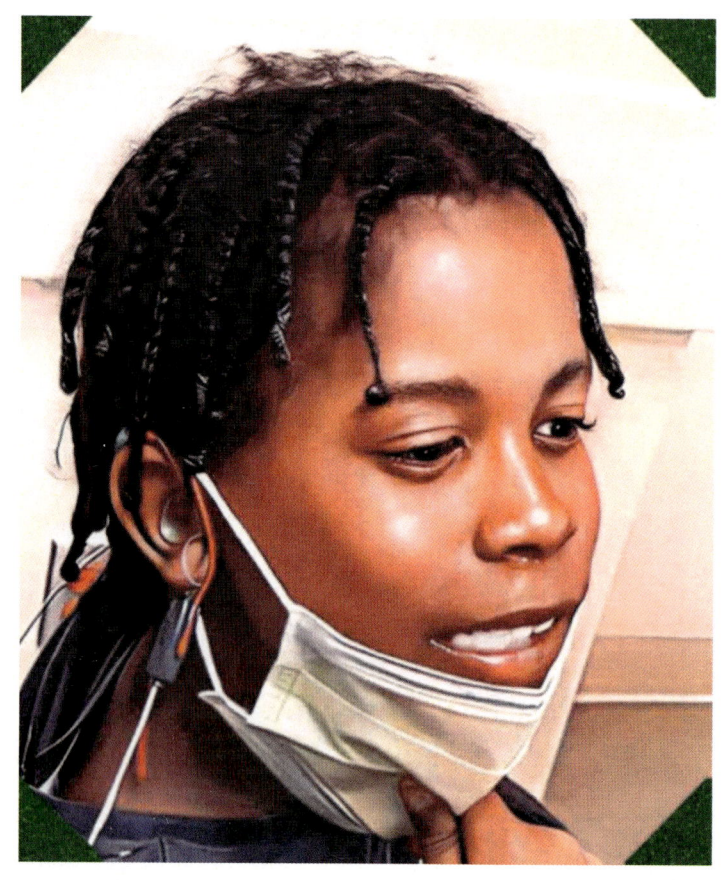

When my aids were ready for pick up, I had to redo the same tests in the soundproof room while wearing my hearing aids to make sure they were running and fitting well. I did not know that this device would change my life forever!

FM SYSTEM

At school, I had to sit in the front of the classroom while my teacher wore an FM hearing system around her neck. The FM system operates like a small radio that transmits speech from a microphone worn by my teacher. The sound is then delivered to my hearing aids.

I did not mind the hearing aids at first, but as I got older I felt uncomfortable wearing them. The device was helping me with my schoolwork and grades, but I felt like it was destroying my social life and image. I was not making any friends; I felt different. I did not look like the other kids or even sound like they did.

My mother would always tell me how important it was to wear my hearing aids and how they would help me in the future. She said that everyone in their life needs some form of help, whether it is in a form of a device or a helping hand. She told me I was special, but I did not feel special.

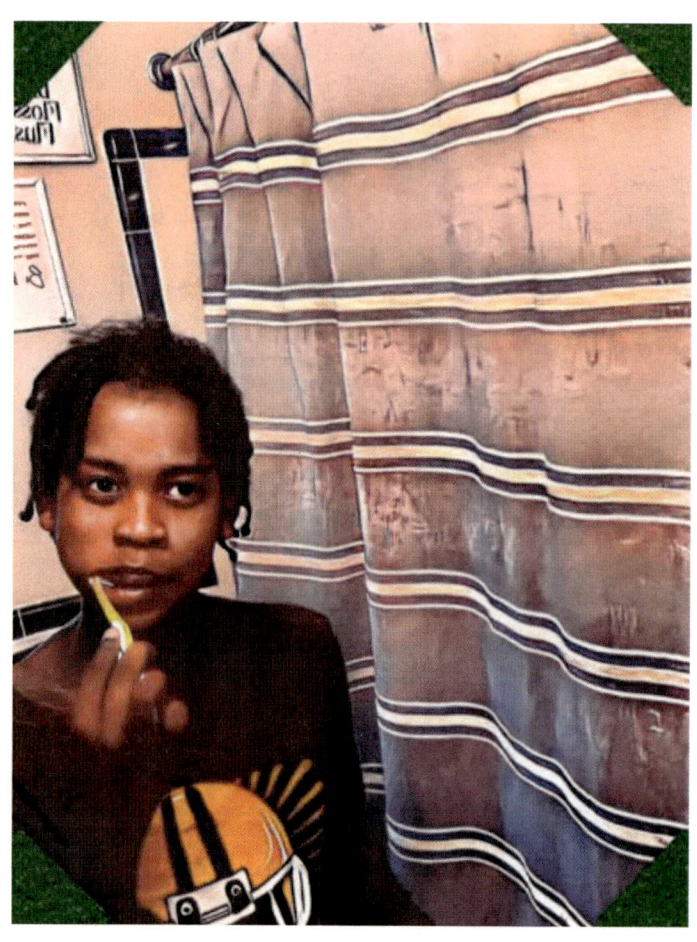

One day things changed for me. It was a regular school day; I remembered waking up to get ready for school. That morning I showered, brushed my teeth, got dressed, put my hearing aids on, and left for school.

Later that afternoon during recess I realized my hearing aids were missing. I was so frantic! As much as I did not like my hearing aids, I knew I needed them. I started searching for them, but it was hard to find on my own. I finally asked my teacher for help. The teacher immediately made an announcement to everyone at recess and told the students that my hearing aids were missing.

Most of the students stopped playing and started helping me look for my hearing aids. A couple of students even made signs that read "Missing Hearing Aids – REWARD: $1.00 or Chocolate Bar." For the rest of our recess, we searched for my hearing aids. When we returned to our classroom, the principal made an announcement encouraging students to return my hearing aids to the office if found.

That week in school, students would spend their recess break helping me look for my hearing aids and others would even come up to me to show me support. I even made friends that week. We never found my hearing aids but that day I did realize something. I realized that I was not alone or as different as I thought I was. All those feelings I had about wearing hearing aids were not true.

My hearing aids were not ruining my life. They were helping me! The hearing aids were part of who I was and a part of my growth. With my hearing aids, I am able to communicate, learn material in school in order to pass my classes, and my peers and loved ones could better understand me.

LEARNING

GROWING

That school year I had confidence in myself. I wore my hearing aids every day. My speech and communication skills improved; I passed my classes and was awarded for my good grades (Distinguished Honors), and I even made a lot of friends. So, yes, I am just like you! I just need a little help. My mom was right all along - I am special.

Hearing and Sound

```
E P T R U S D N S W R I N G I N G
L C J A T N A E F P E A C F Q V A
I M H X A O J C E A E S M P R Q V
S N B O T I N G R Y V E K M D A D
T T O S W T A Q J L G I D X E G P
E T A I Z A R B P V D N S X N B I
N I N S T R U M E N T O I I E U T
I M H H D B V S M G U N R Z P T C
N K U A Q I I L I N C A E J Z B H
G Y Z H M V B E D C E G B U E U P
B S A M J Z R B W H J F B M L R B
M Z L F Q E A I K E L C U E D O O
D R G E V I T C G G X L O N H Z W
X O V A V H E E Y A O E N E M B W
U Z W X W A G D Q V C R X R B H W
K J W K T K R I K H X K S G B E N
F Z L Z V N Z T H Q N S Z Y J O X
```

ENERGY	RINGING	SPEED	WAVE
TRAVELS	HIGH	VOLUME	PITCH
EAR	HEARING	BUZZING	ECHO
LOW	SOUND	LISTENING	VIBRATE

Write about a time when you felt different:

Write about a time someone helped you:

Write about a time you helped someone:

Write about a time someone made you feel special:

ABOUT THE AUTHOR

Semaj Lopez was born in the city of Philadelphia, Pennsylvania. He was a premature baby born in a "coma vigil" state. Semaj's medical obstacles included seizures, moderate hearing loss, and speech impairment. As a toddler, Semaj had to take physical and speech therapy at least four times a week.

Today, Semaj can move freely and speak clearly, and is no longer required to take medication for seizure episodes. He may have to wear hearing aids, but that does not stop him from being who he is destined to be.

Semaj is now a Distinguished Honor student, loves to play sports (mainly basketball and football), and enjoys spending time with his family and friends. Semaj Lopez hopes to inspire others with special needs and to embrace their lives as well.

Made in the USA
Middletown, DE
21 October 2022